◆

INNER GAME OF SUCCESS

QUOTES TO GET YOU THERE

Ebony D. McPherson

◆

Copyright © Ebony D. McPherson, 2024

All rights reserved

No part of this book may be reproduced, stored in a retrieval system, or transmitted in any form by any means, electronic, mechanical, photocopying, recording, or otherwise, without express written permission of the publisher

Except in the United States of America, this book is sold subject to the condition that it shall not, by way of trade or otherwise, be lent, re-sold, hired out, or otherwise circulated without the publisher's prior consent in any form of binding or cover other than that in which it is published and without a comparable condition including this condition being imposed on the subsequent purchaser

Cover design by: Ebony D. McPherson

Printed in the United States of America

CONTENTS

Chapter 1   BUILD……………..……....…1

Chapter 2   INCREASE…………….……...17

Chapter 3   REGENERATE……..….…….33

Chapter 4   ENRICH……………..………..49

Chapter 5   CULTIVATE …….….……......65

Chapter 6   REFINE……………..……....81

Chapter 7   REFOCUS………............…..97

Chapter 8   SUCCESS…………...……..…111

Resources   ……………..……………..125
About Author   ……..………………….....127

DEDICATION

For the builders

1

BUILD

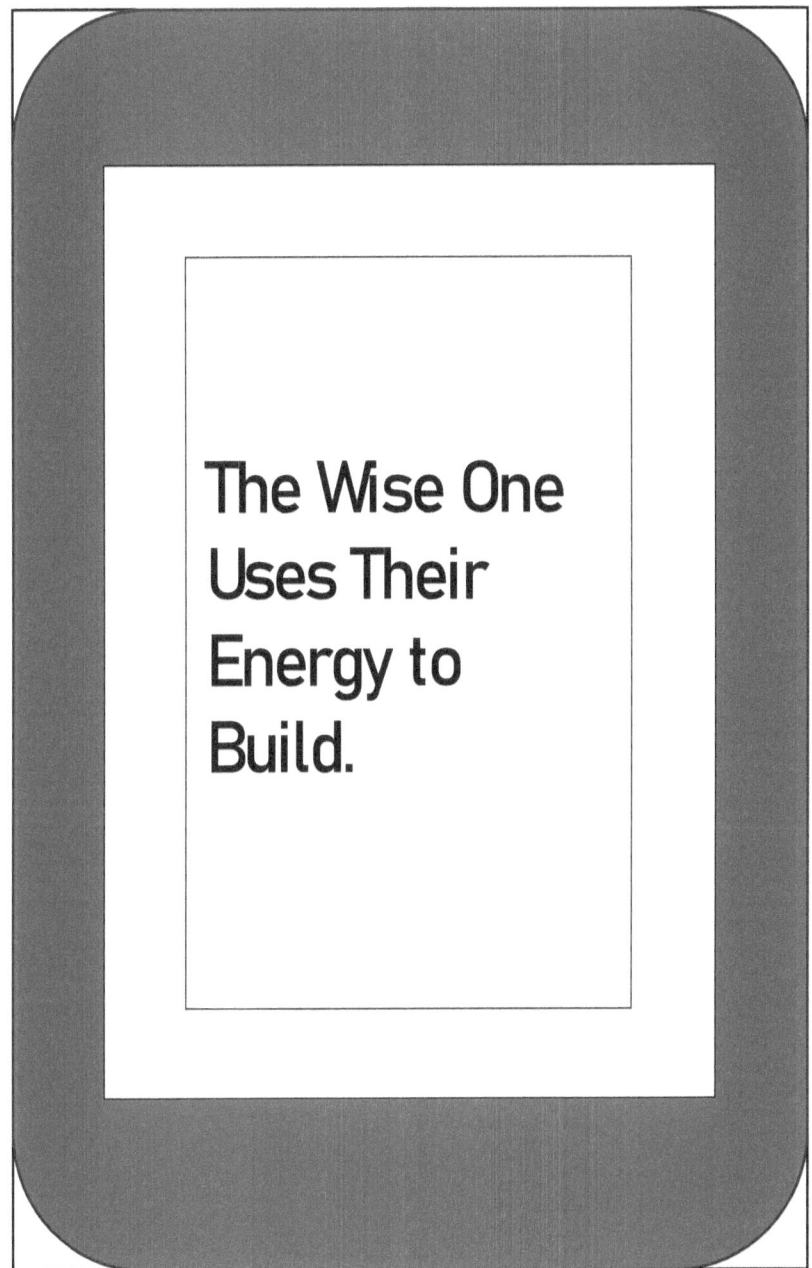

The Wise One Uses Their Energy to Build.

EBONY D. MCPHERSON

Master the Art of Becoming.

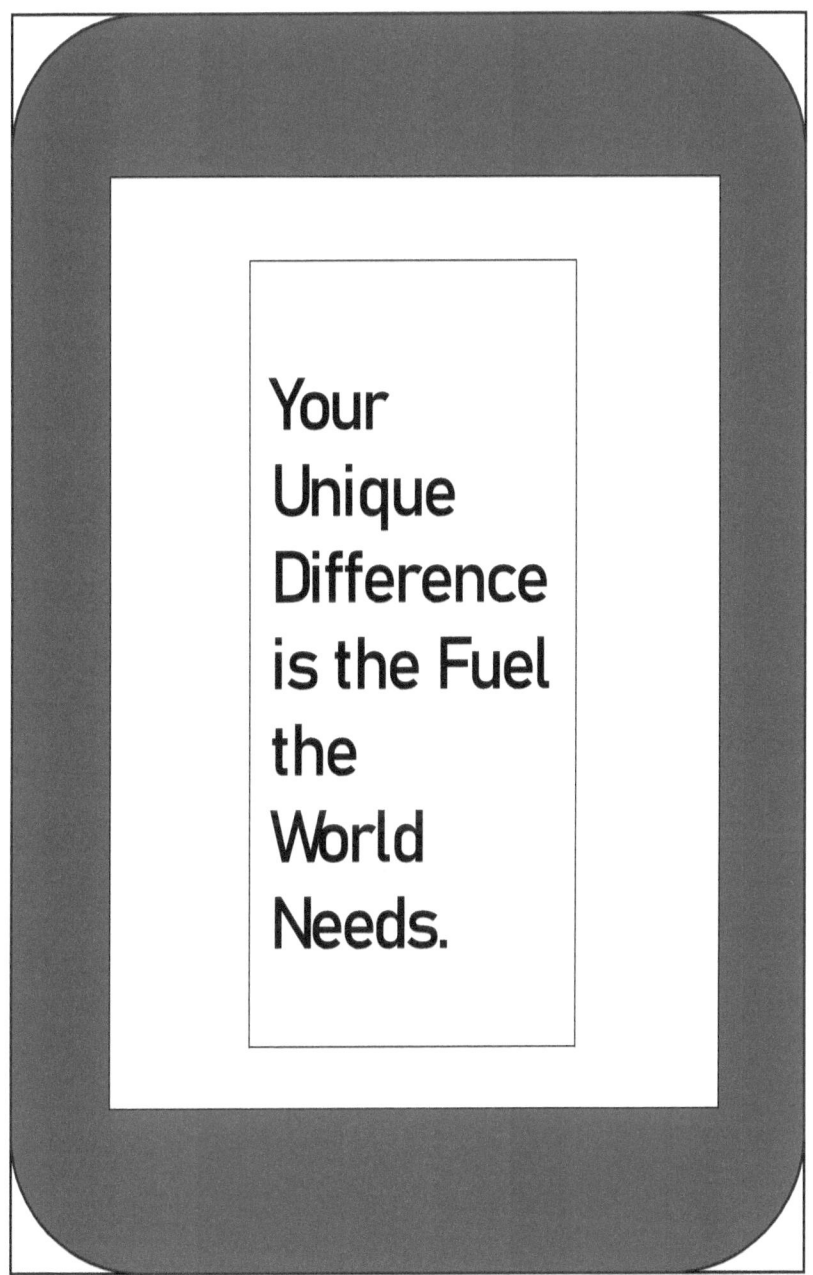

EBONY D. MCPHERSON

Use Your Life to Write Your Dreams.

BUILD

Find
Strength in

Action.

EBONY D. MCPHERSON

Do More with Less.

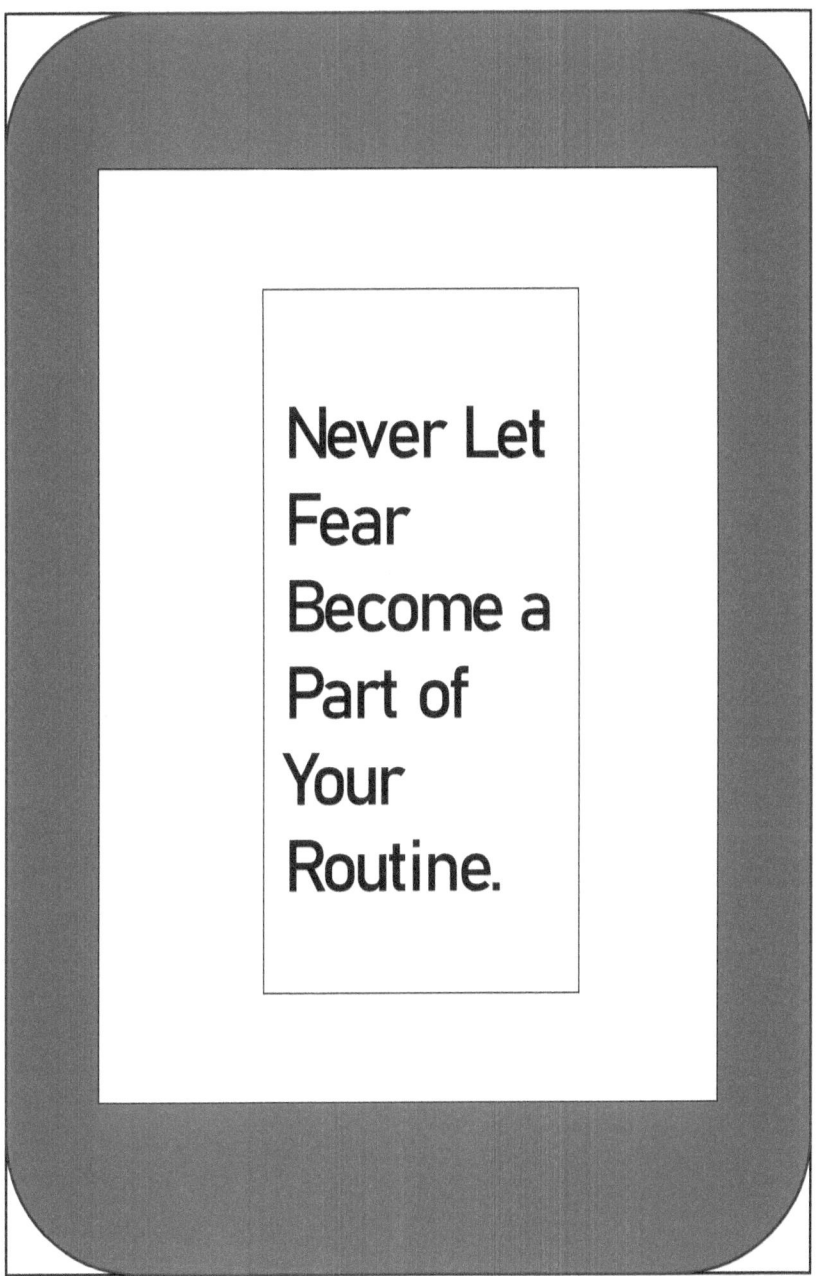

A Little Effort in Each Day will Go a Long Way.

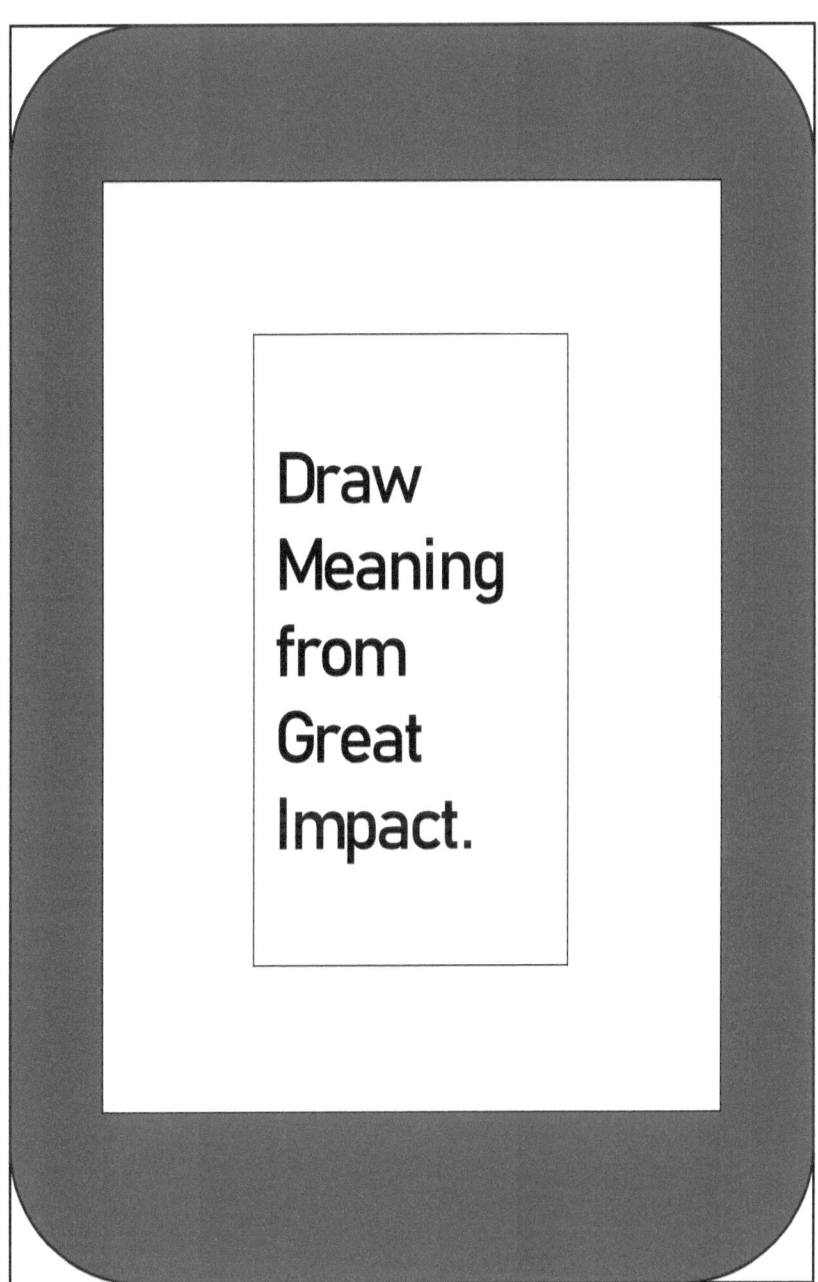

You Can Increase Your Potential by Increasing Your Performance.

Inspire Harmony with Each Life You Touch.

Enrich Life with Wise, Heartfelt Decisions.

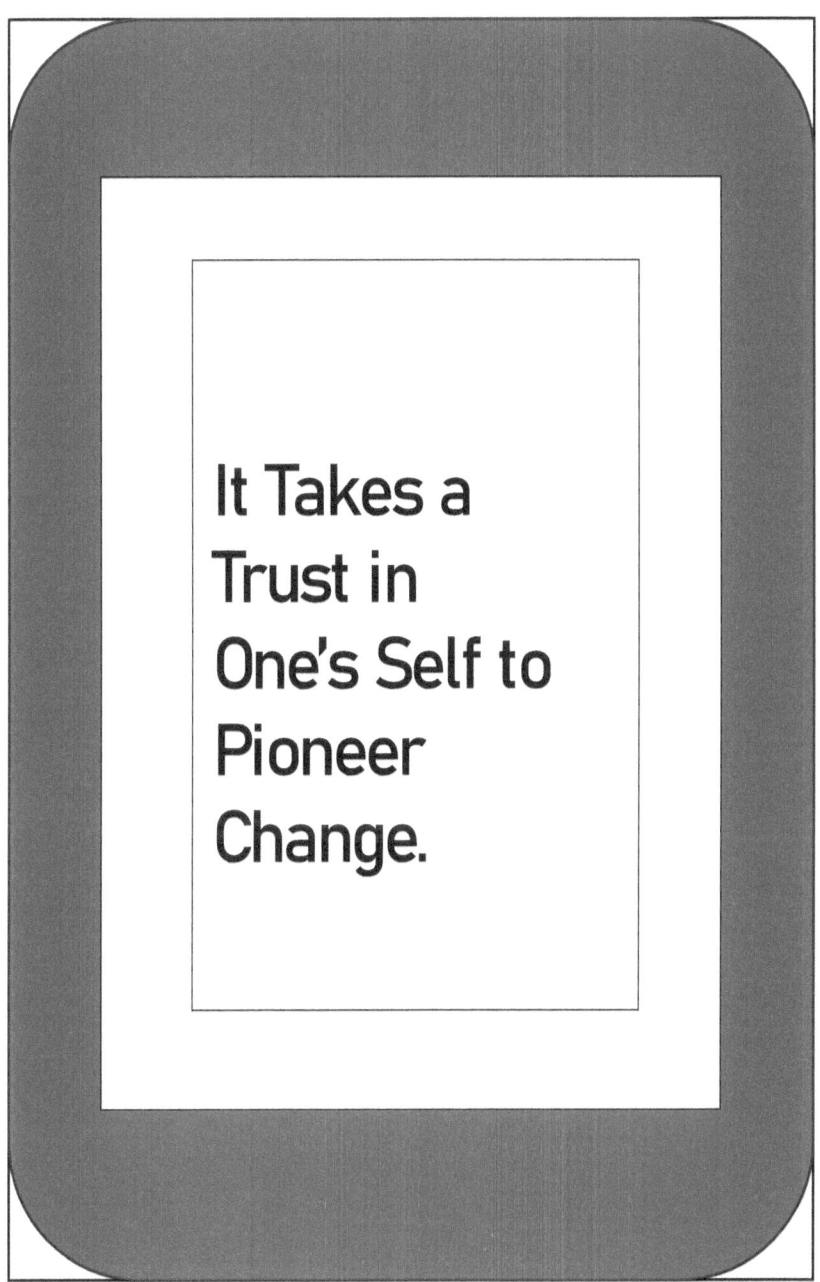

It Takes a Trust in One's Self to Pioneer Change.

2

INCREASE

INCREASE

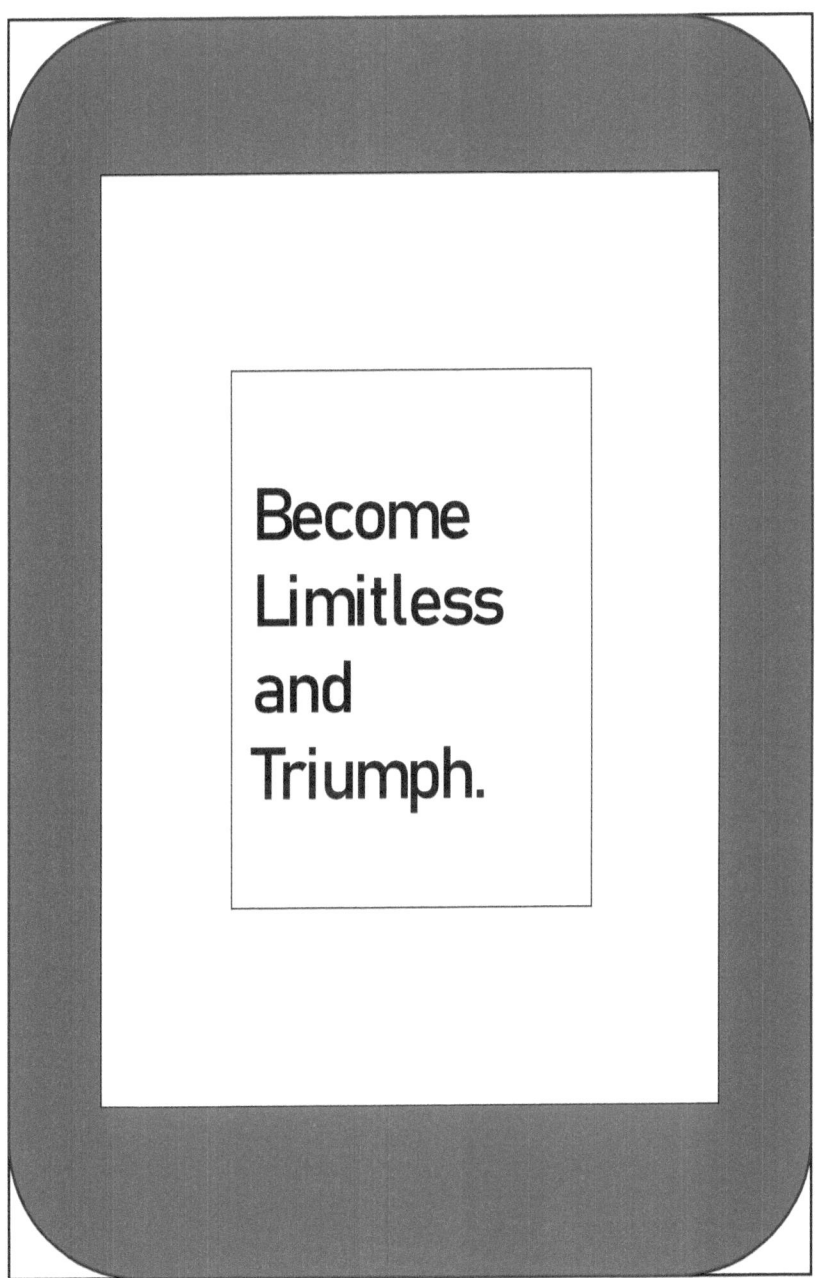

Never Be the One to Place Limits on Your Own Success.

INCREASE

Sometimes Less Effort Produces More.

A World-Class Perspective Can Lead to Frequent Wins.

Hope with Diligent Works Makes Dreams Come True.

INCREASE

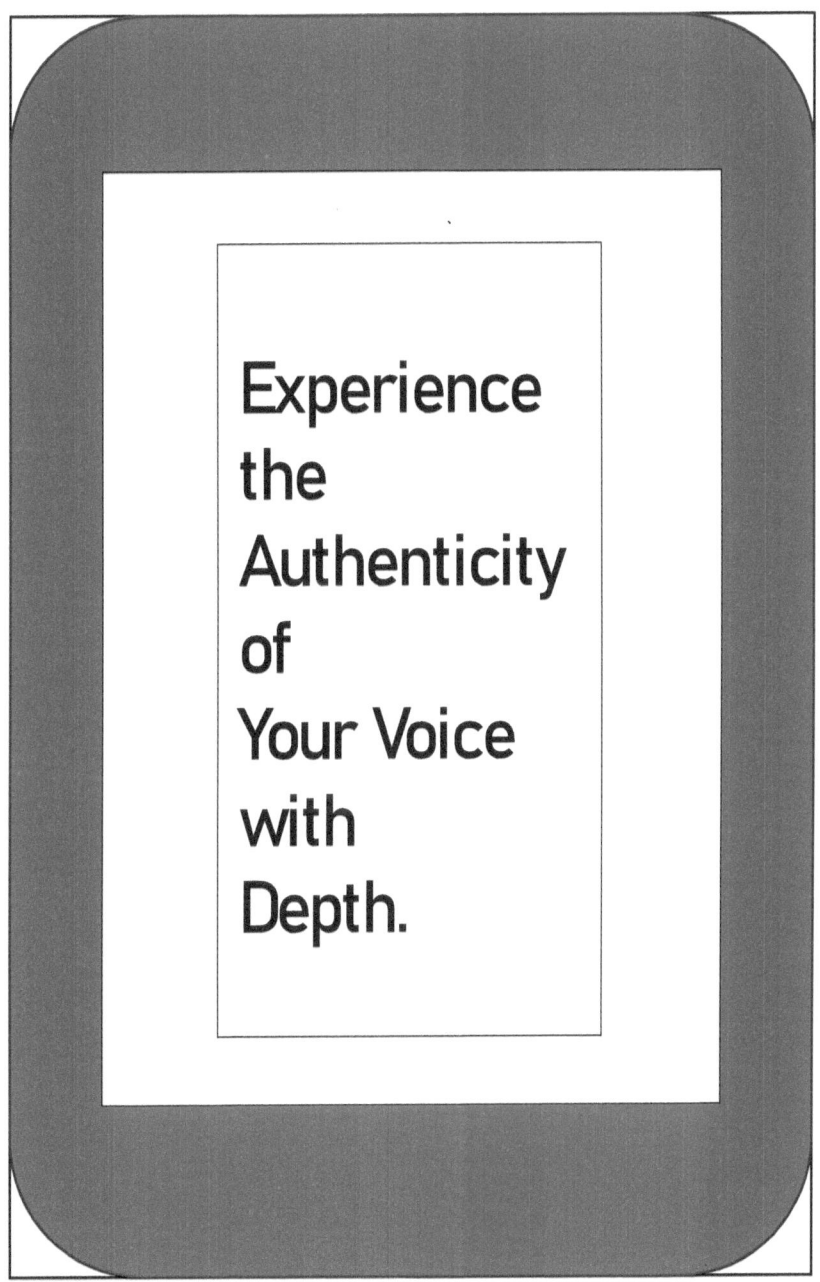

Experience the Authenticity of Your Voice with Depth.

EBONY D. MCPHERSON

Character is the Greatest Currency of Life.

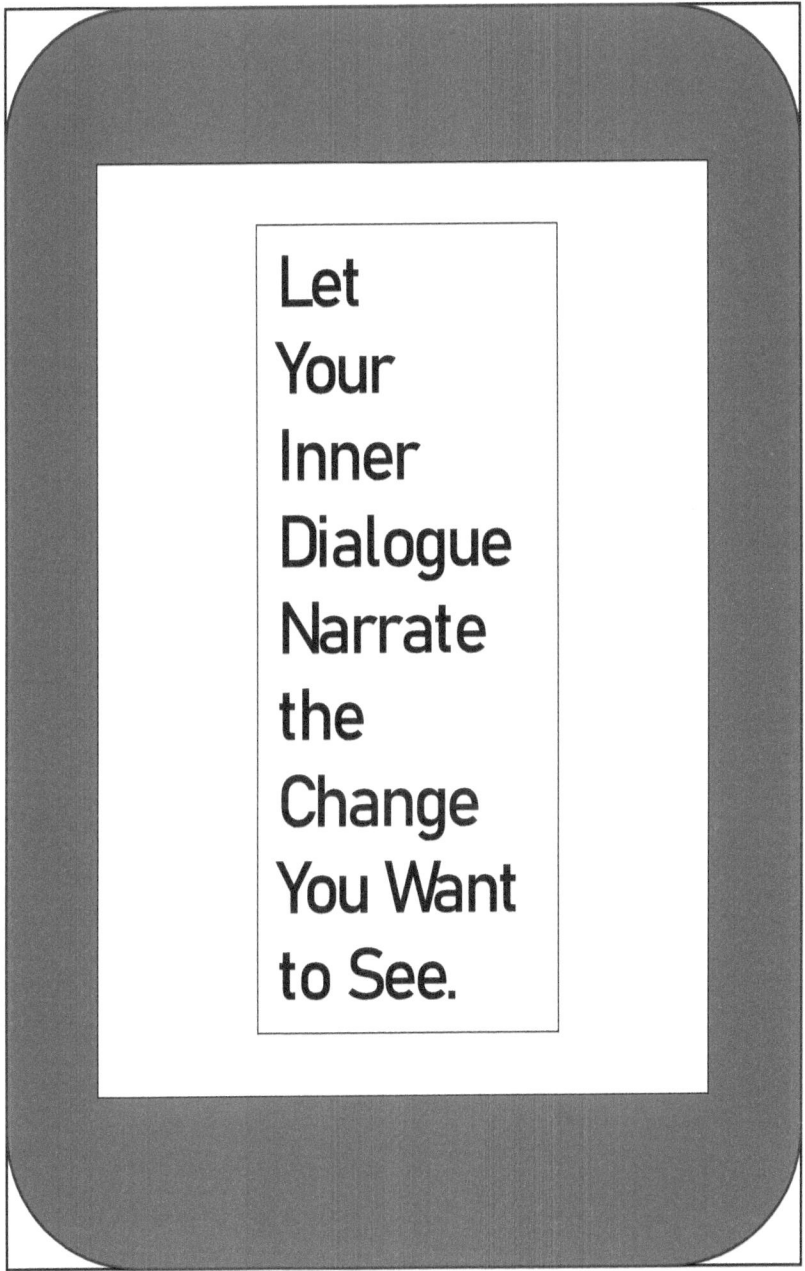

Let Your Inner Dialogue Narrate the Change You Want to See.

Give Yourself Grace when Pioneering the Unknown.

INCREASE

In Your Mind Lies the Freedom to Dream Infinitely.

INCREASE

Endurance Meets the Goal.

3

REGENERATE

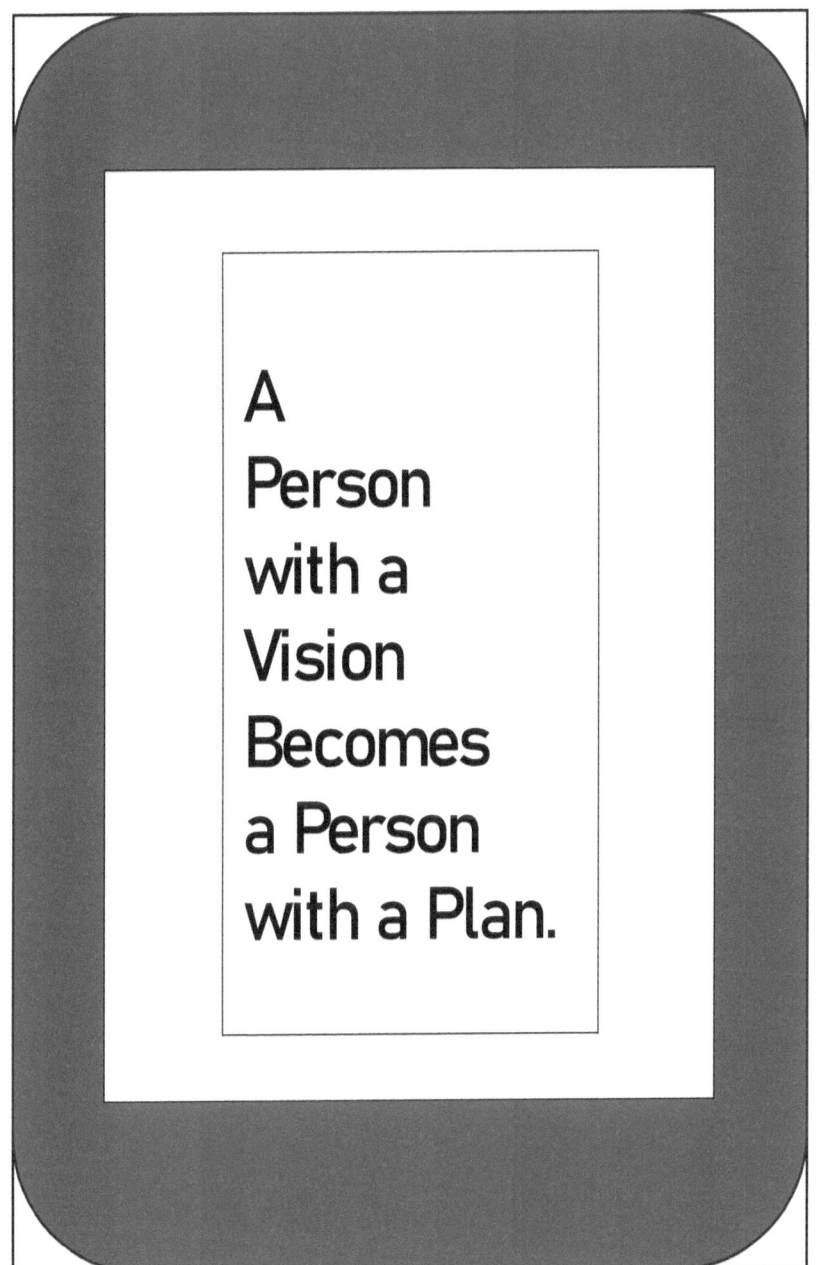

Promises Made with Compassion Reveal Strength in Character.

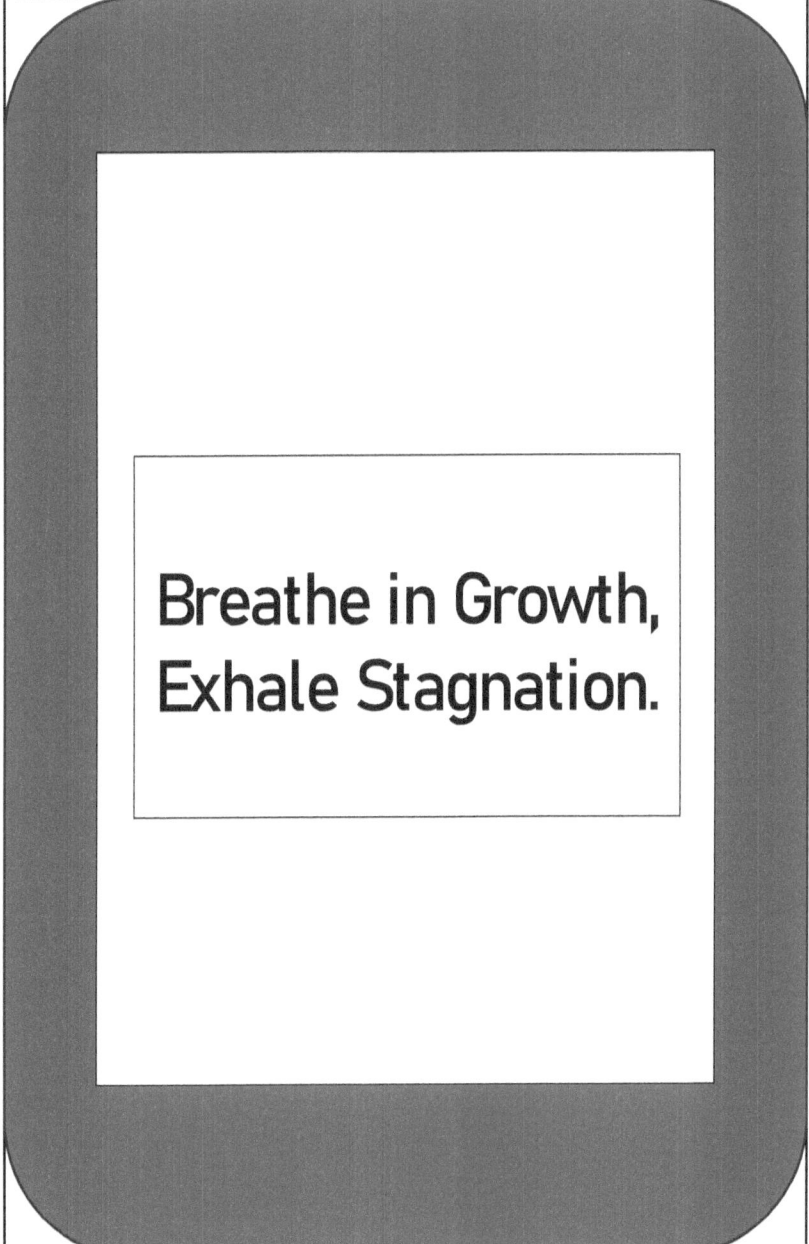
Breathe in Growth, Exhale Stagnation.

A Strong Mind Makes Peaceful Decisions.

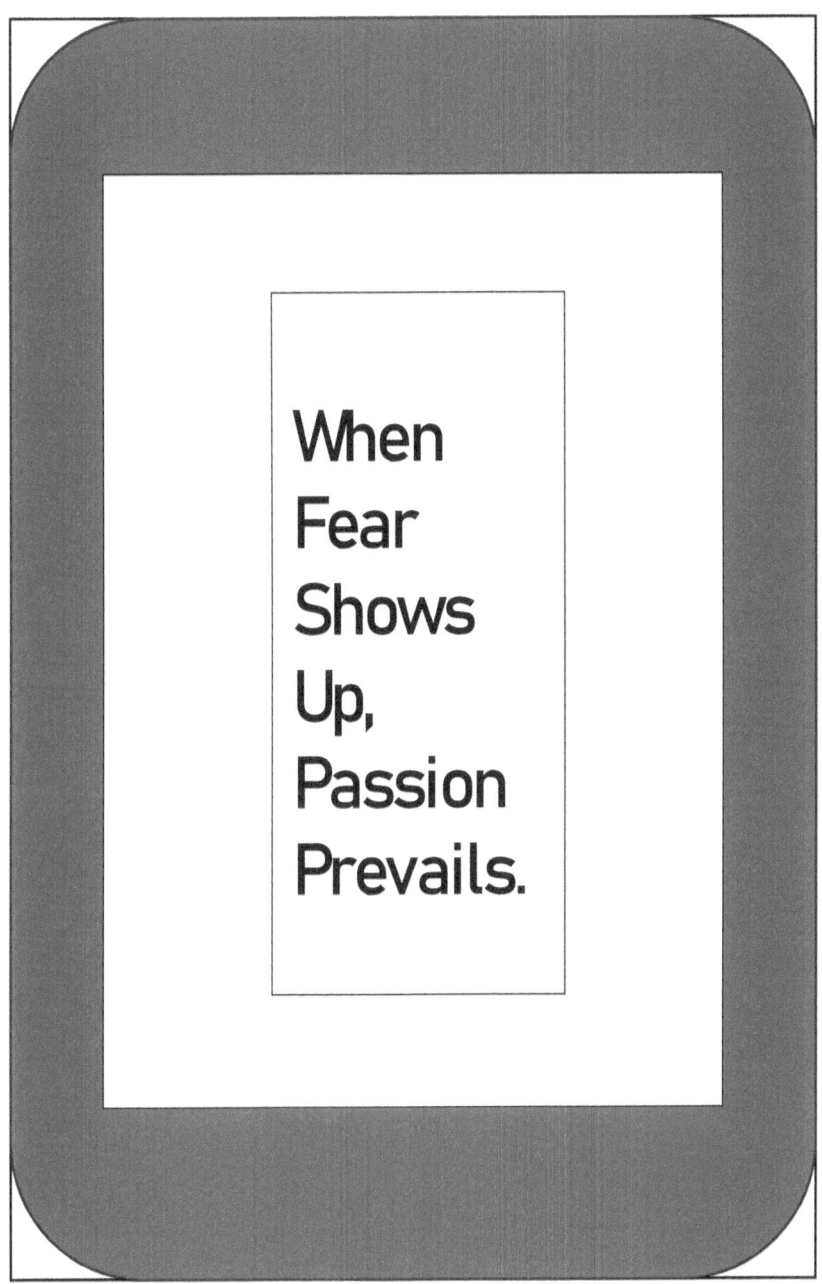

Never Give Up Hope While Disciplining Your Choices.

REGENERATE

Never Underestimate an Opportunity to Reset and Start Again.

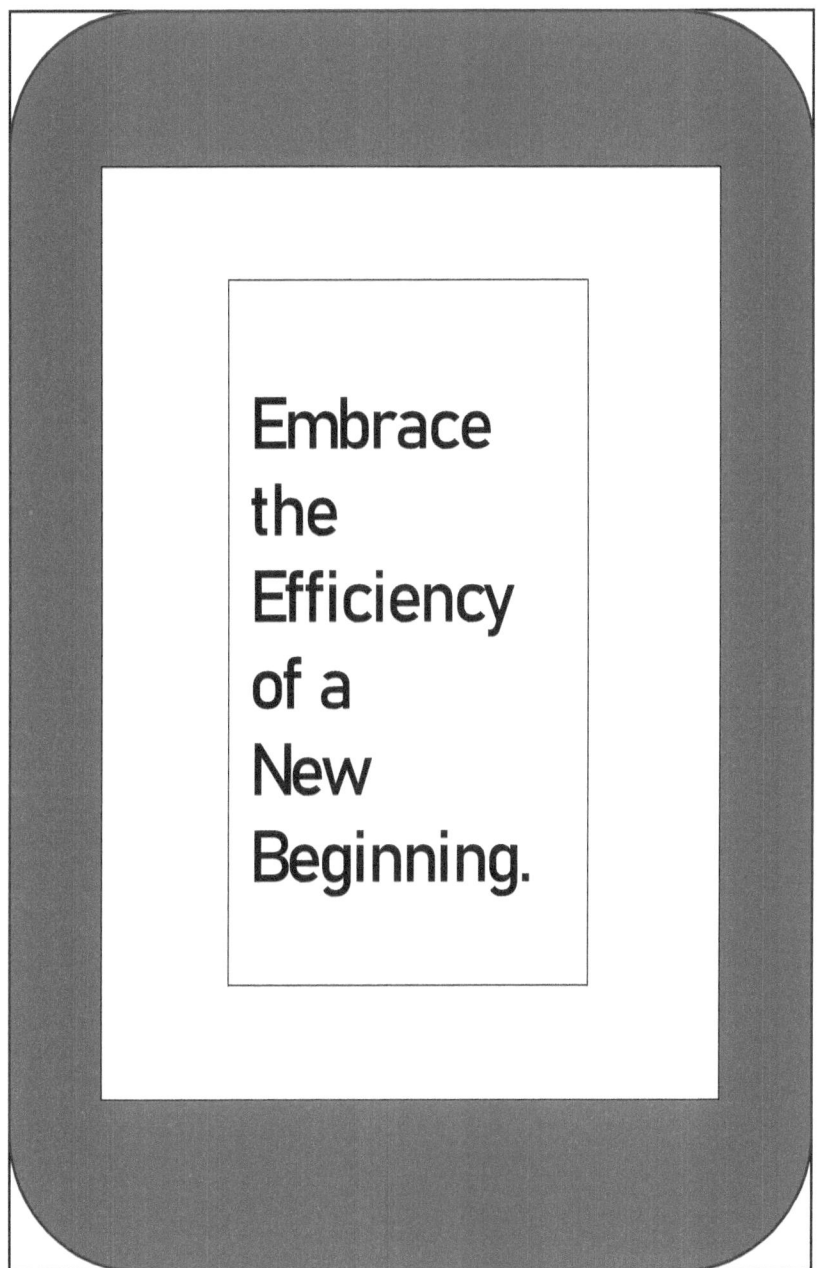

EBONY D. MCPHERSON

Bring Flair to Your Articulated Thoughts.

The Grass is Indeed Greener Where You Water It.

Be Guided by Your Inner Grace.

REGENERATE

Your Reflection is Infinite.

4

ENRICH

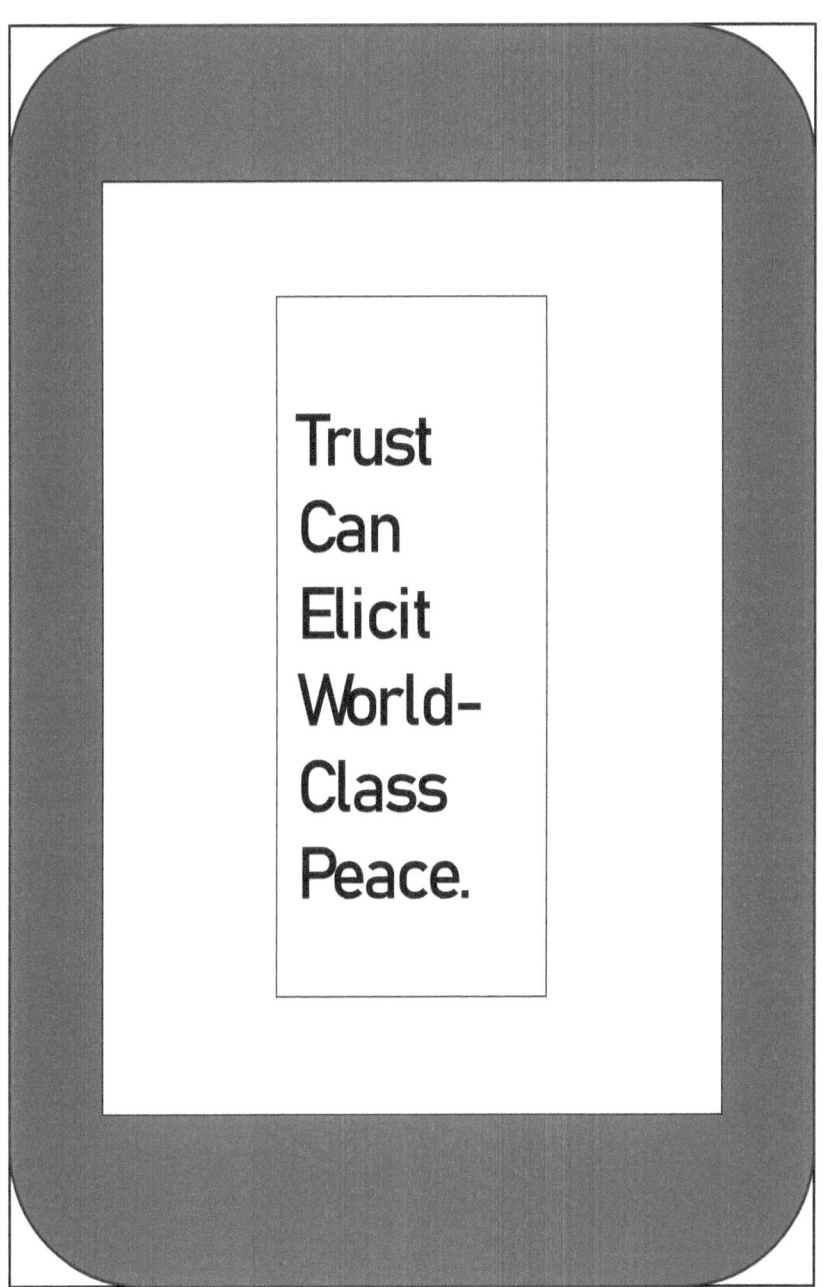

Trust Can Elicit World-Class Peace.

A Deeper Knowledge of Self Allows a Deeper Impact for Change.

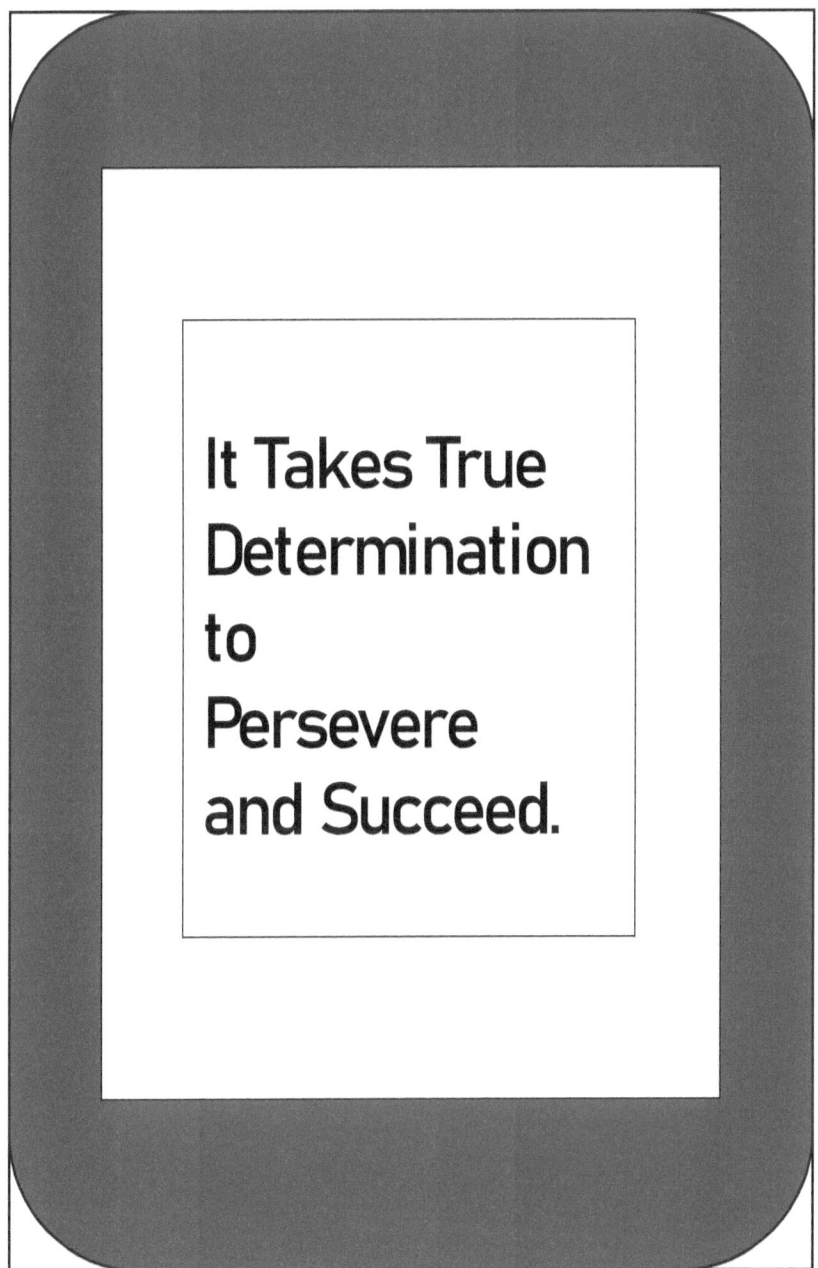

> *Never Regret Mistakes Along the Way in Attempt to Chase Your Dreams Courageously.*

The Abundance of Epiphanies Create a Strong Mind.

A True Gift is Friendship that Encourages Achievement.

Reflect Often on Perspectives that Have the Power to Change the World.

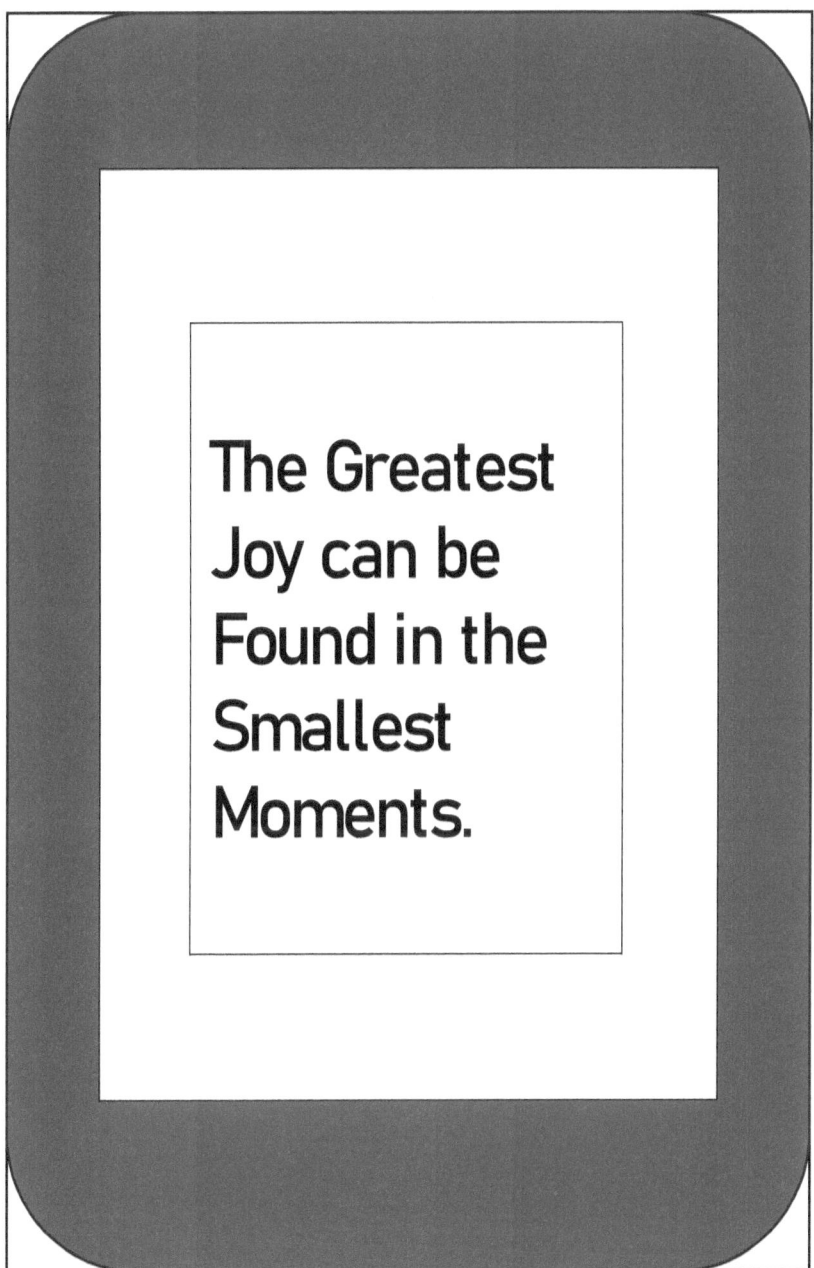

The Greatest Joy can be Found in the Smallest Moments.

A Simple Act of Kindness can Bring Abundant Peace.

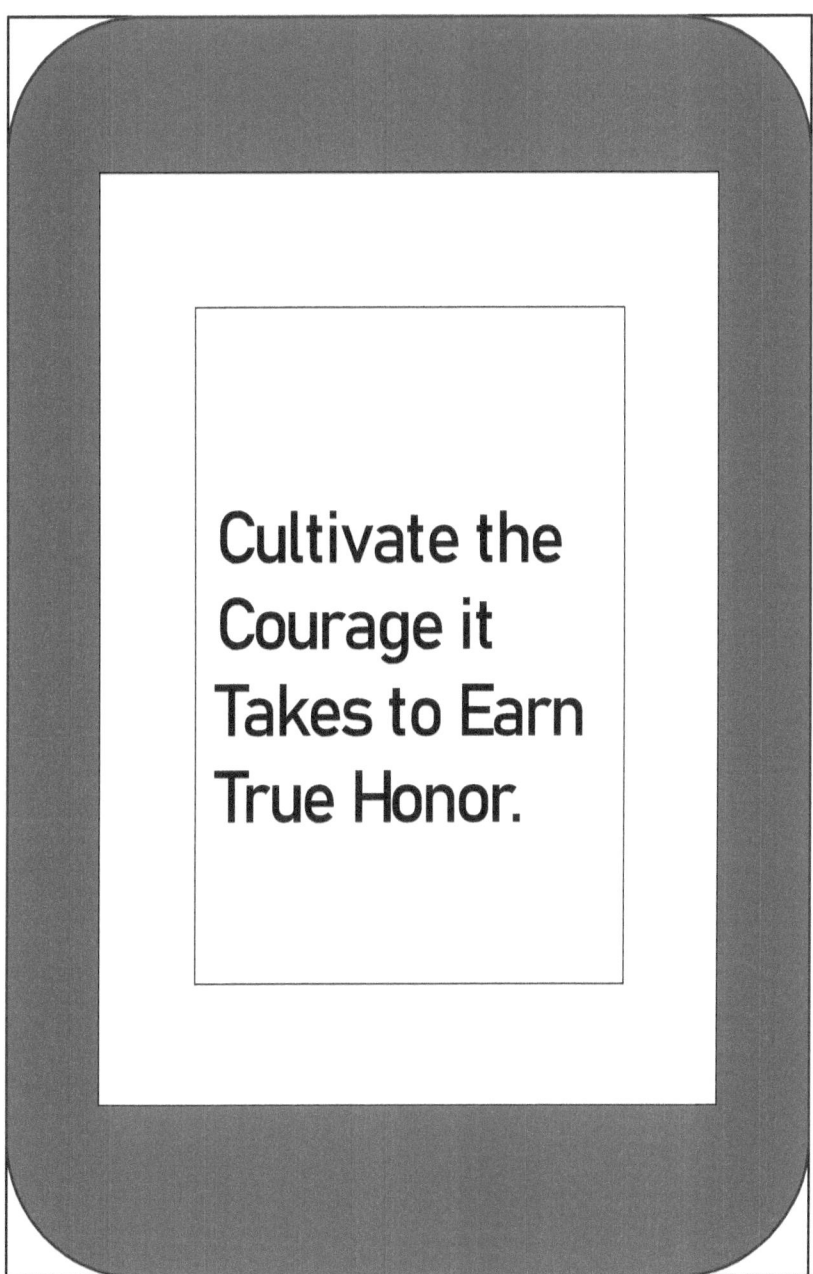

Cultivate the Courage it Takes to Earn True Honor.

Never Lose Sight of the Gift Your Uniqueness Creates.

If We Shine Together, those that are Farther Away Can See Us.

5

CULTIVATE

Perfection is in Balance of Heart and Mind.

EBONY D. MCPHERSON

Never Let the Seed of Fear Grow.

Use Courage to Lean into the Part of You that Does Not Fit in the Box.

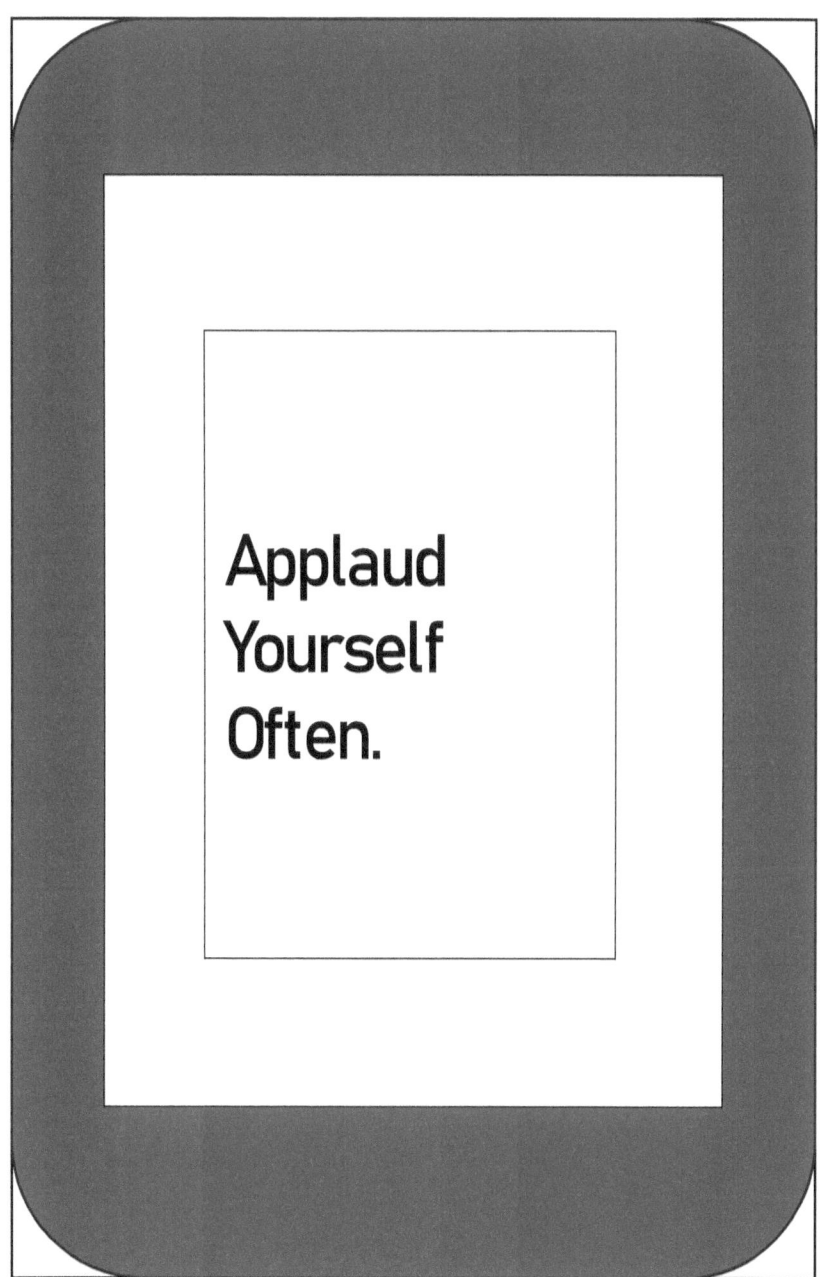

EBONY D. MCPHERSON

Knowing Yourself Can Open Doors for Others.

CULTIVATE

The Greatest Goal One Can Create is One that Brings Peace.

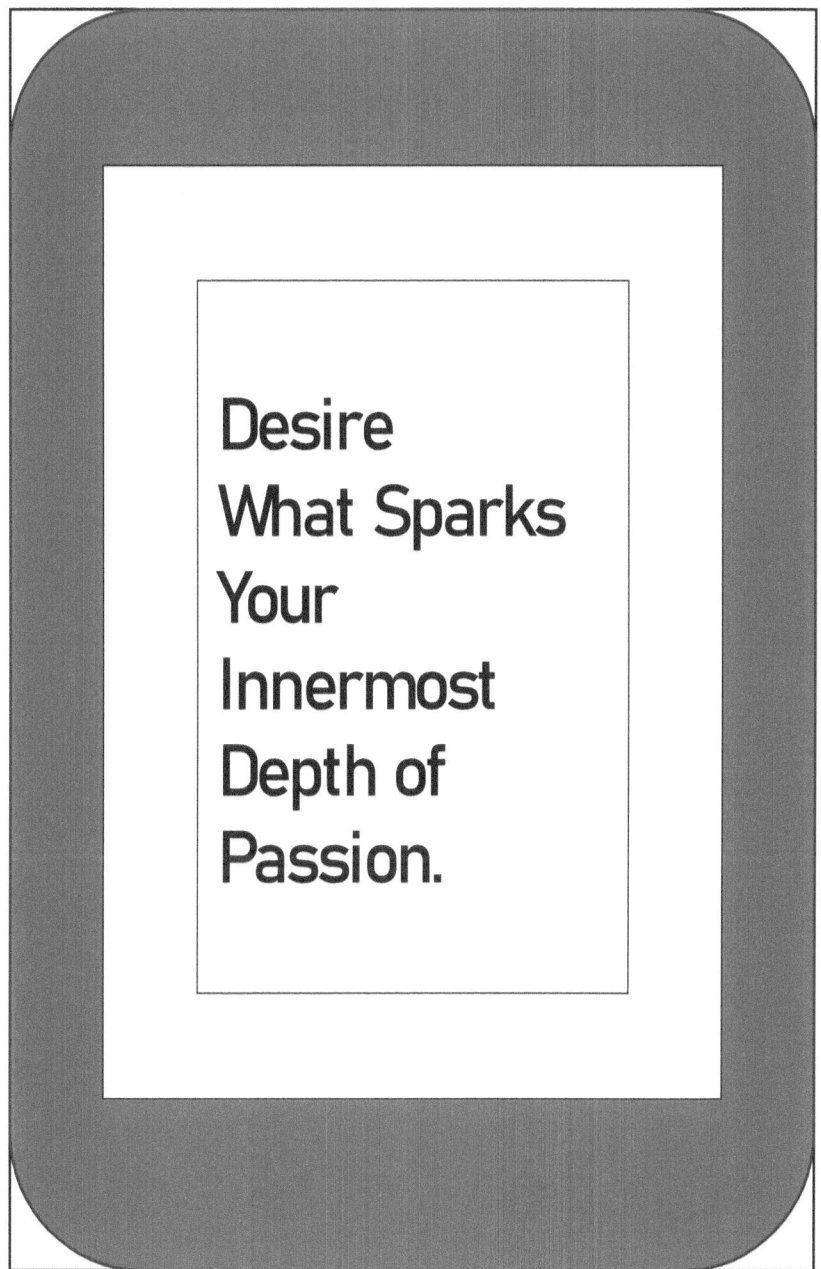

Desire What Sparks Your Innermost Depth of Passion.

Allow the Journey to Carve the Memorable Moments.

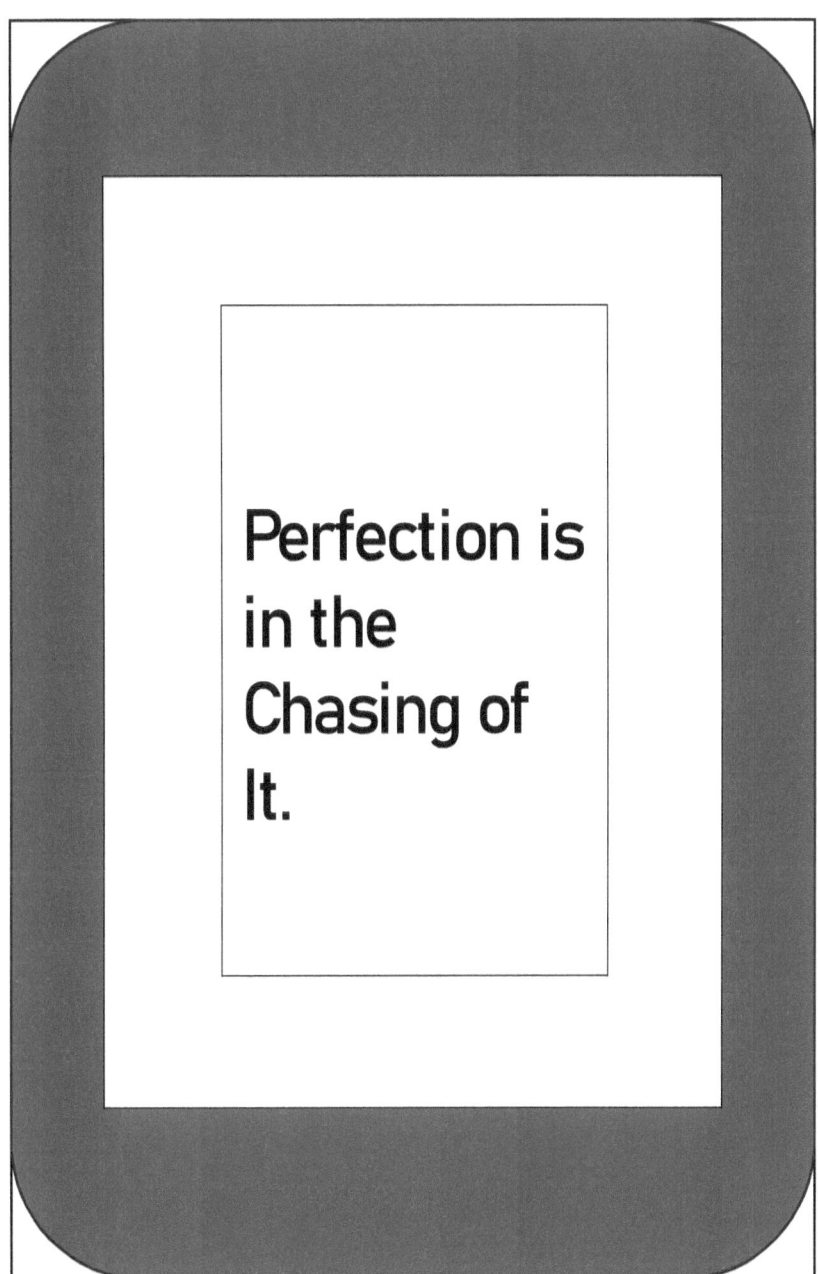

Perfection is in the Chasing of It.

Anticipation is a Great Place to Practice Discipline.

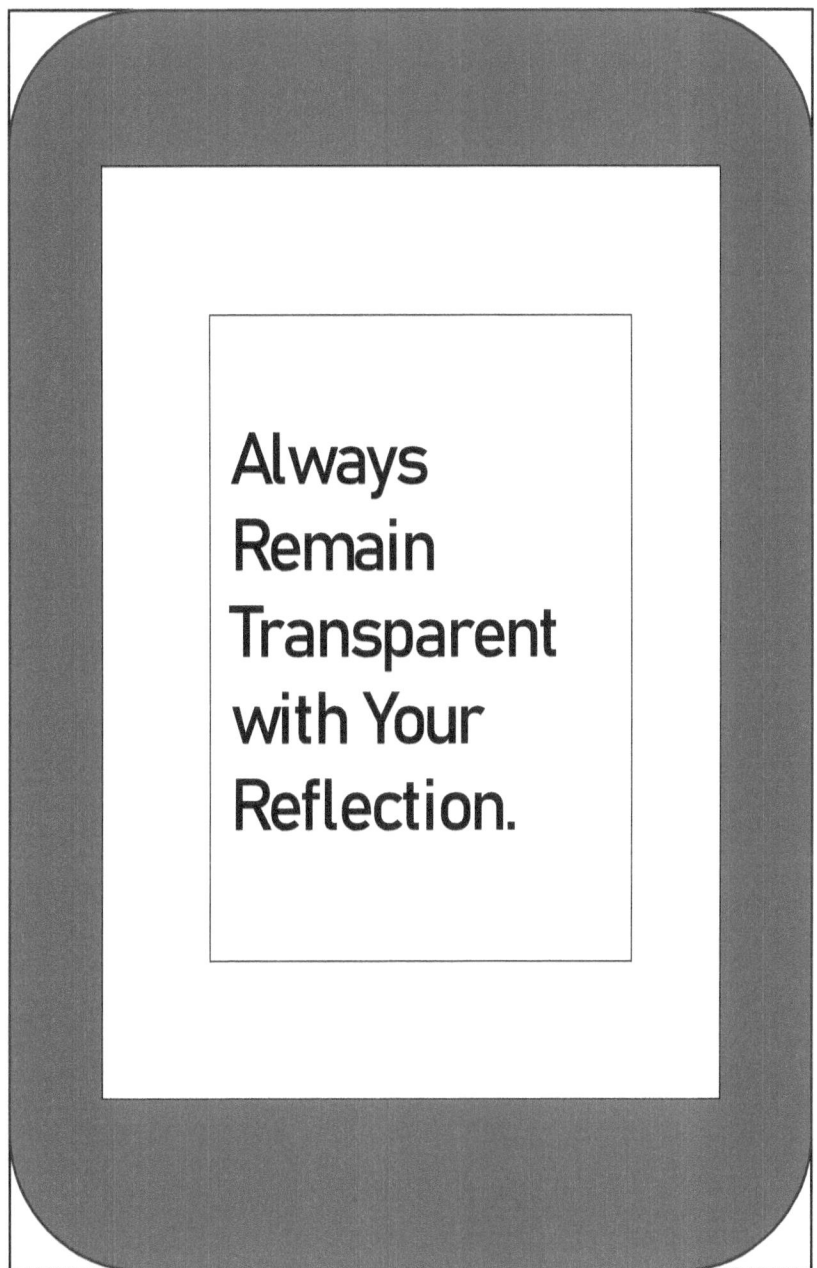

Always Remain Transparent with Your Reflection.

6

REFINE

REFINE

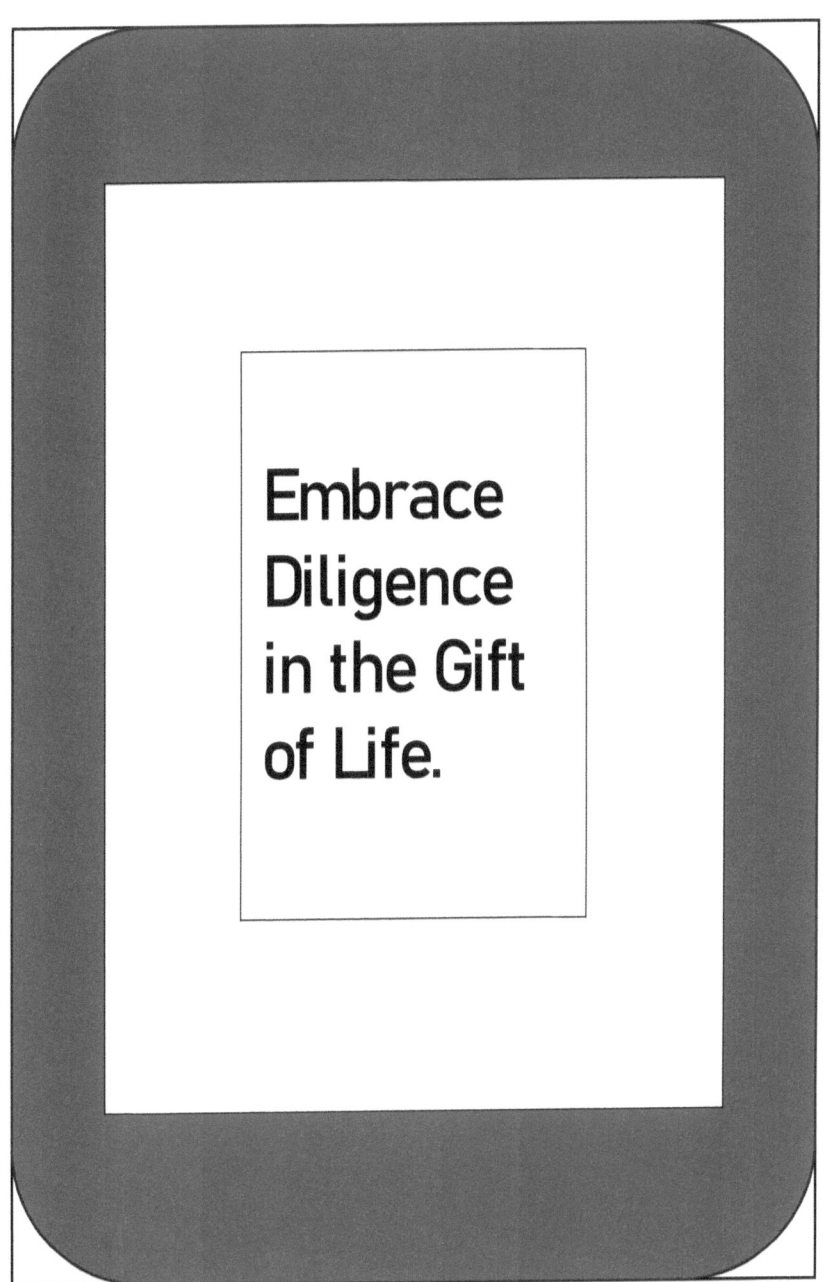

Embrace Diligence in the Gift of Life.

Fuel Your Dreams with Unwavering Ambition.

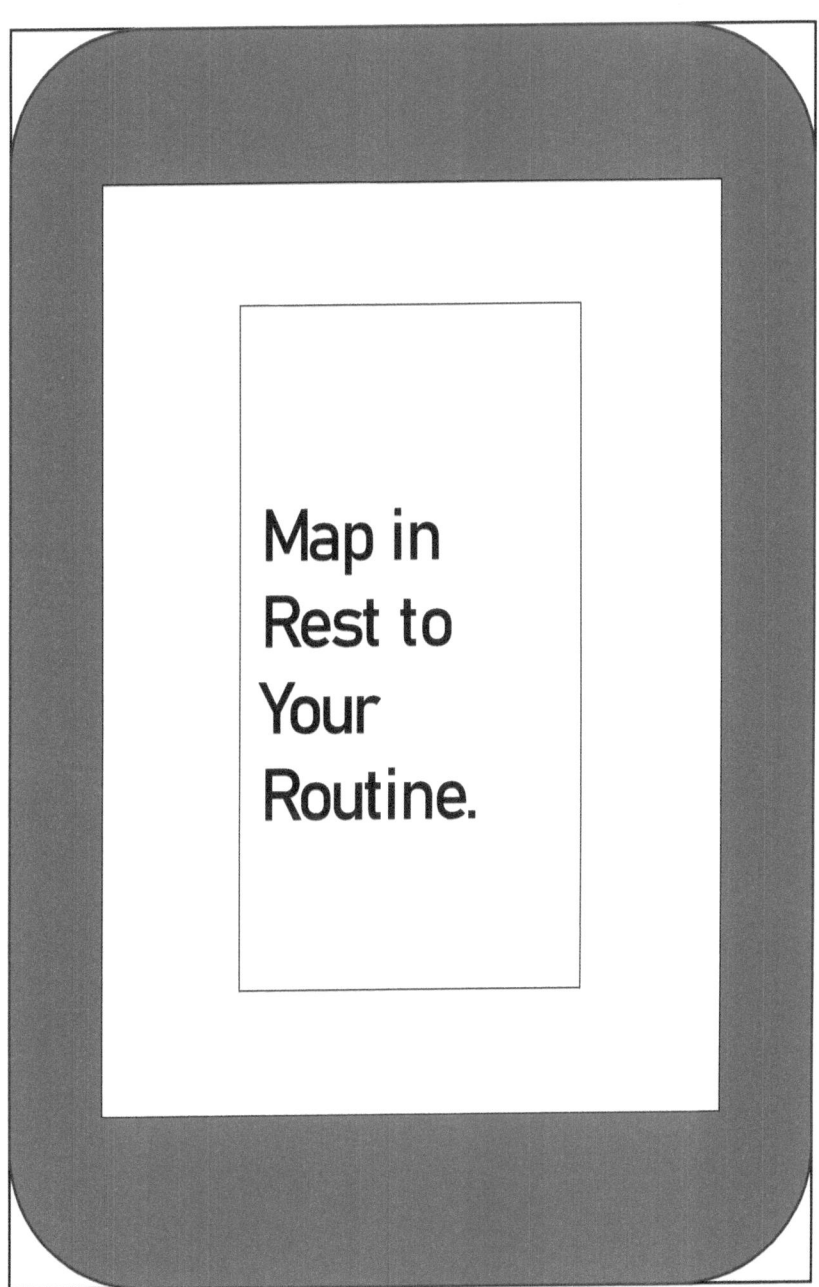

The Turbulence in Life is What Increases Strength.

REFINE

Happiness Often Sticks Close to Gratitude.

EBONY D. MCPHERSON

Sophisticated Courage Can Bring Sweat to the Brow.

A Rainbow in the Clouds to an Eye, is Unity in Harmony to the Heart.

REFINE

Walk into the Unknown with Grace.

Generations Will Thank You for the Endurance You Apply Today.

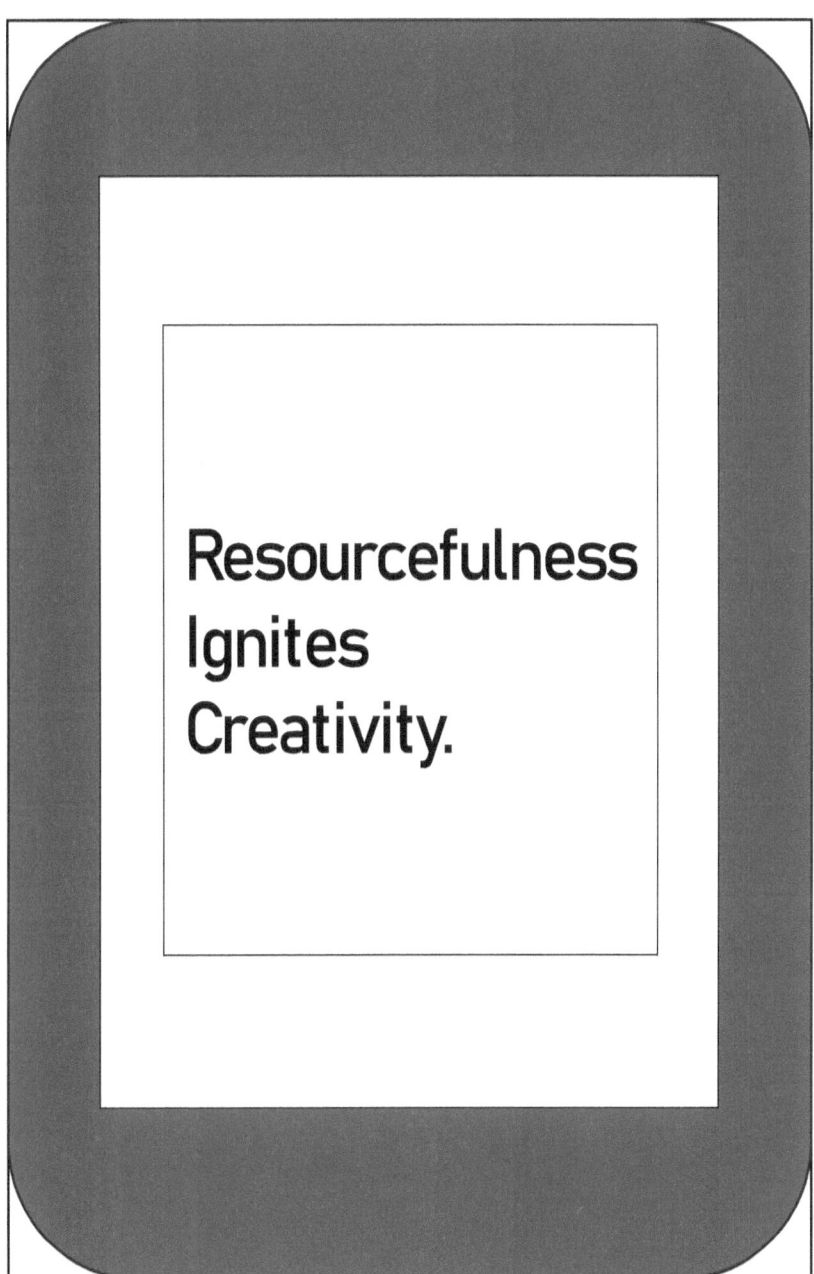

7

REFOCUS

Mindset is Where Everything Important Begins.

Travel Through Life Enwrapped in Progress.

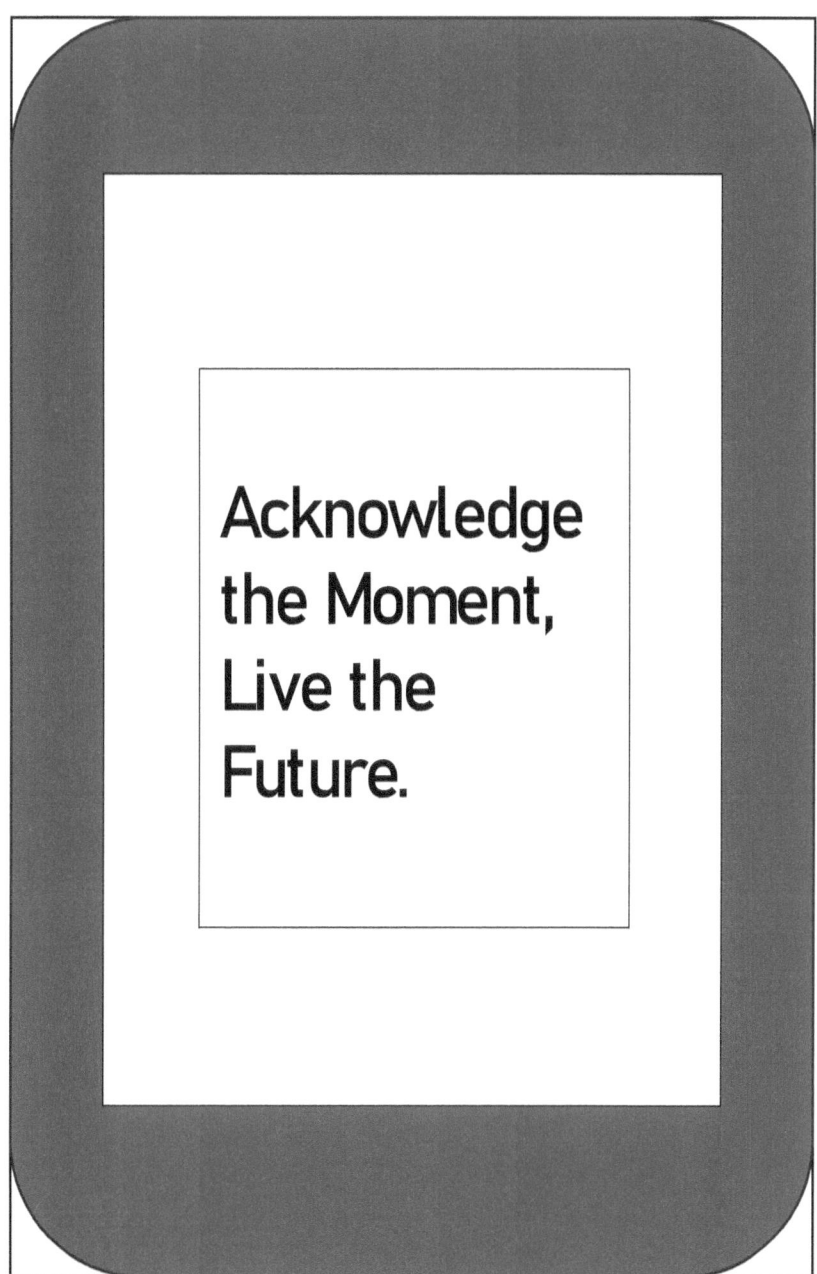

Most Valuable Lessons are Found in Places You Least Expect.

The Best Person to Hold You Accountable is You.

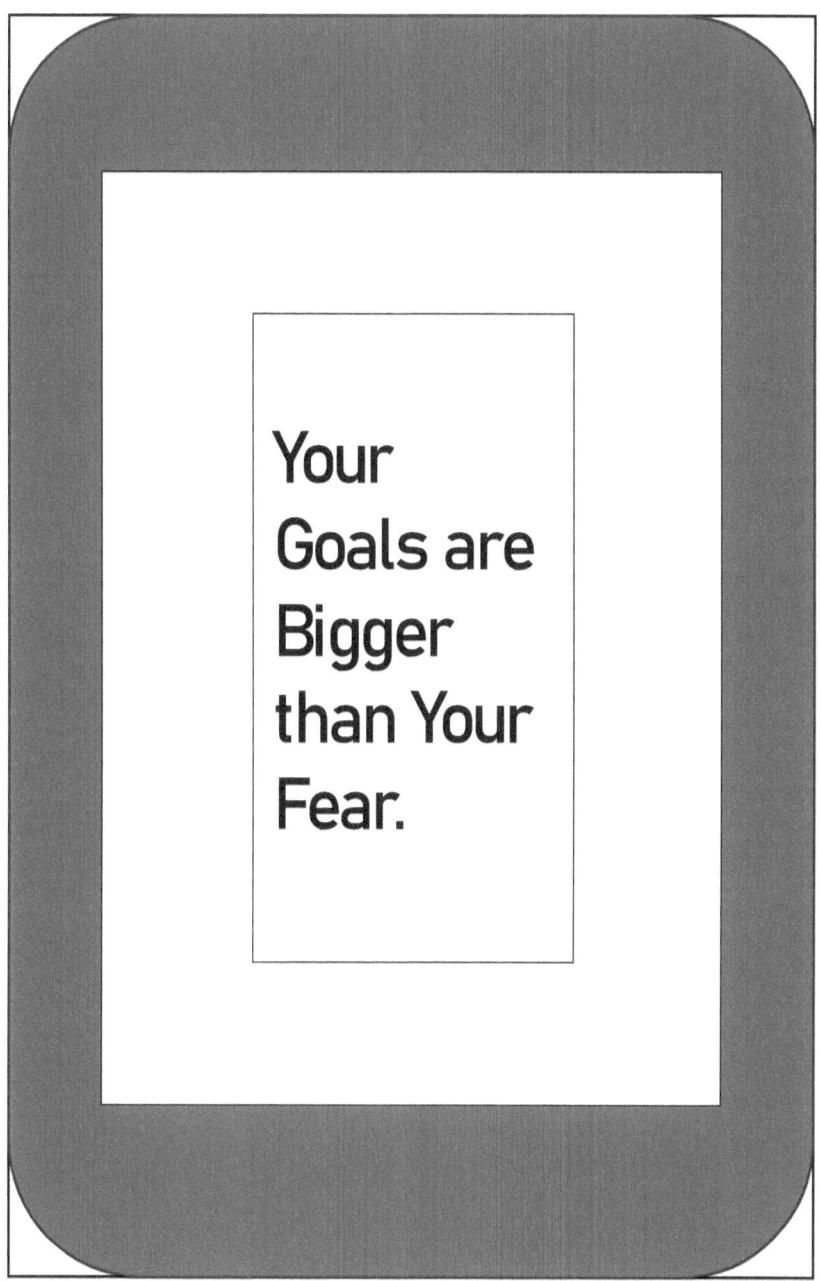

One Who Receives Riches has the Choice Between Amplifying Joy or Grievances.

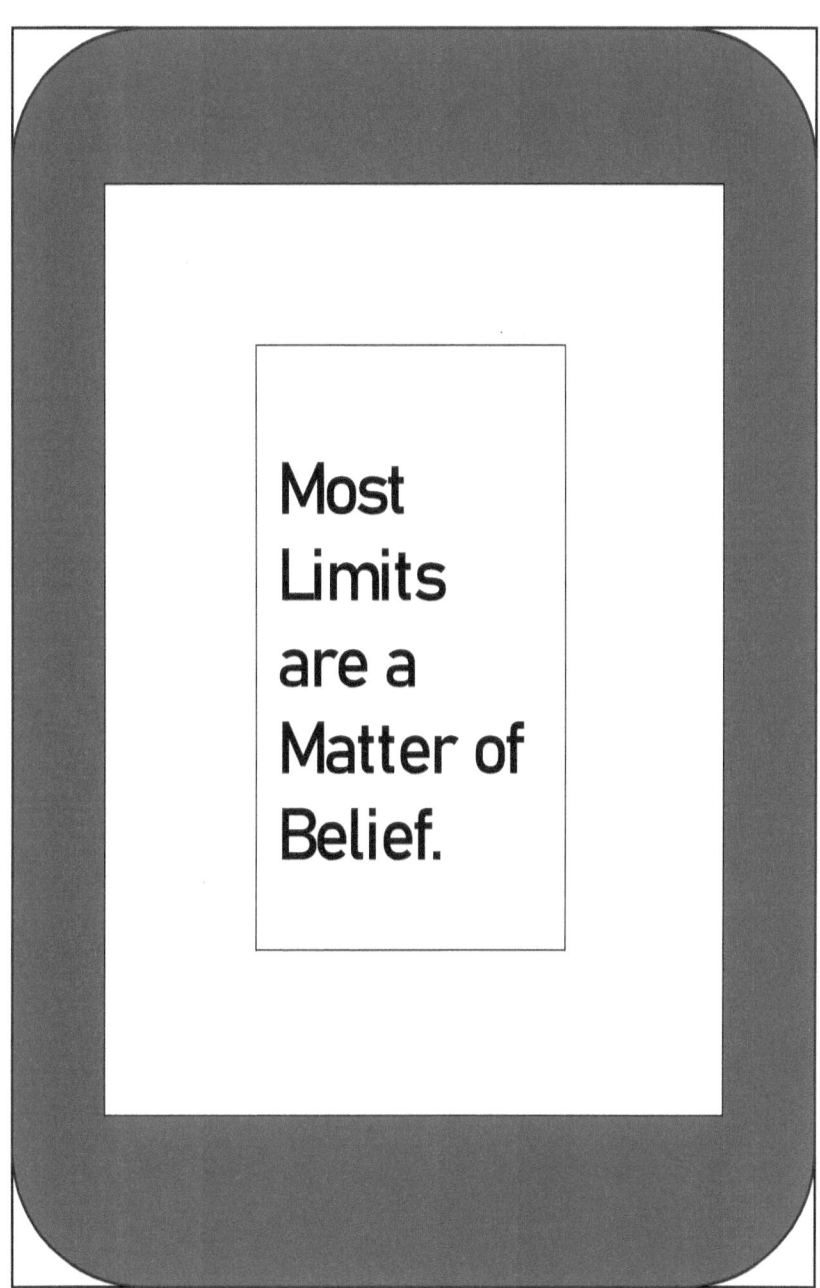

Most Limits are a Matter of Belief.

There is No Limit to Possibilities When You Continuously Have an Idea About an Idea.

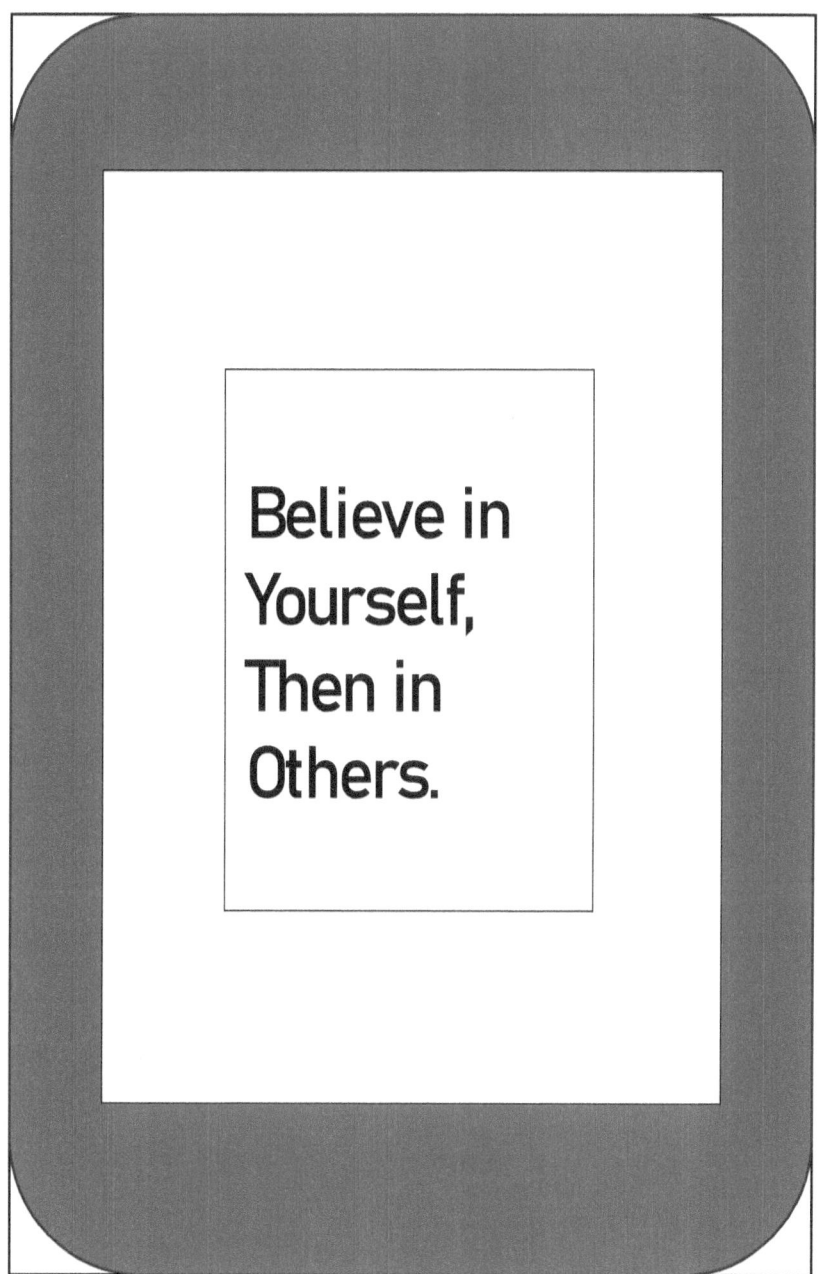

Destiny is Closely Related to Your Uniqueness.

8

SUCCESS

Forgive the Past,
Mind the Present,
Map the Future.

> *Your Experiences have the Power to Propel Future Generations.*

SUCCESS

Be the One that Perseveres.

The Goal of Life is to Consciously Be a Part of Something that Lasts.

SUCCESS

Sometimes it Only Takes a Little to Enjoy a Lot.

Leave Behind Something to Be Distinguished By.

Continuously Chase the Limitless Version of You.

The Greatest Return on Investment into Your Future is Peace.

SUCCESS

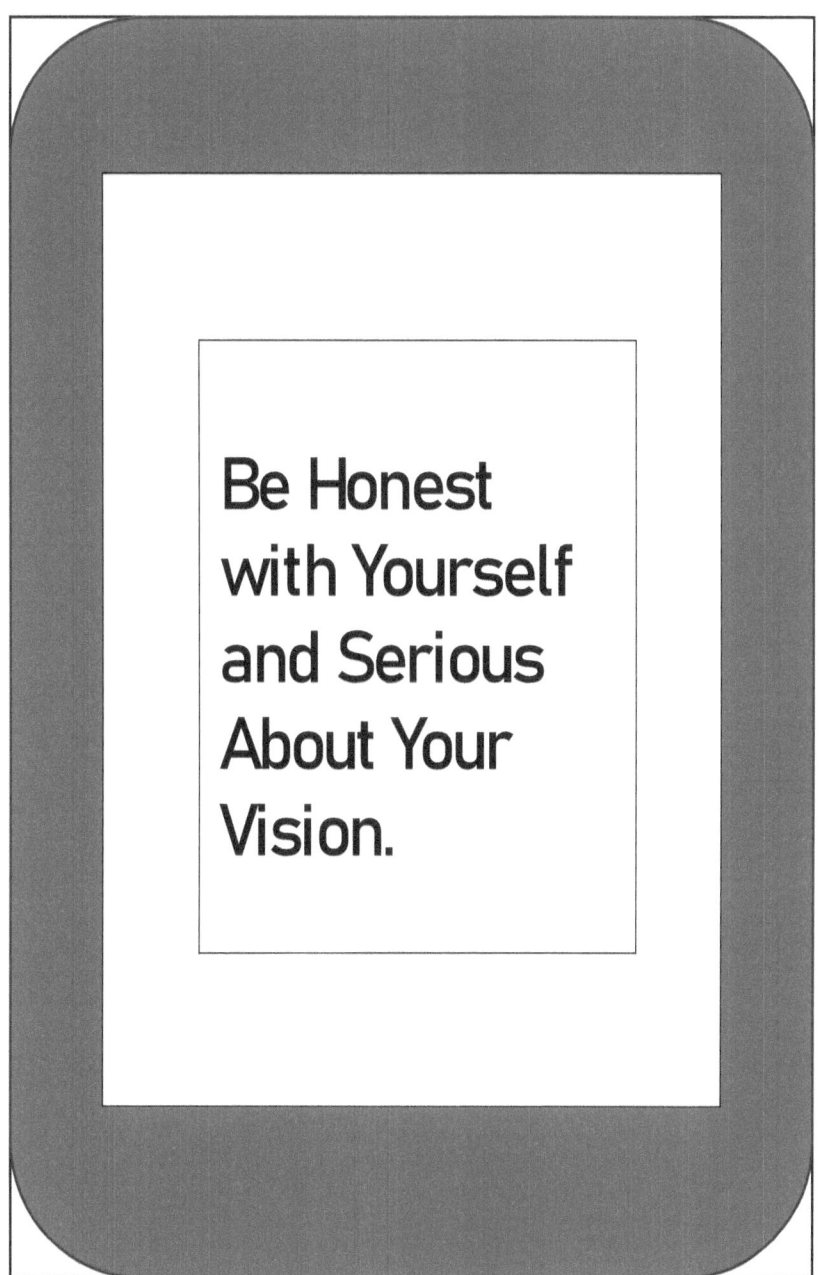

Be Honest with Yourself and Serious About Your Vision.

Acknowledge the Rules, Understand the Players, Master the Game.

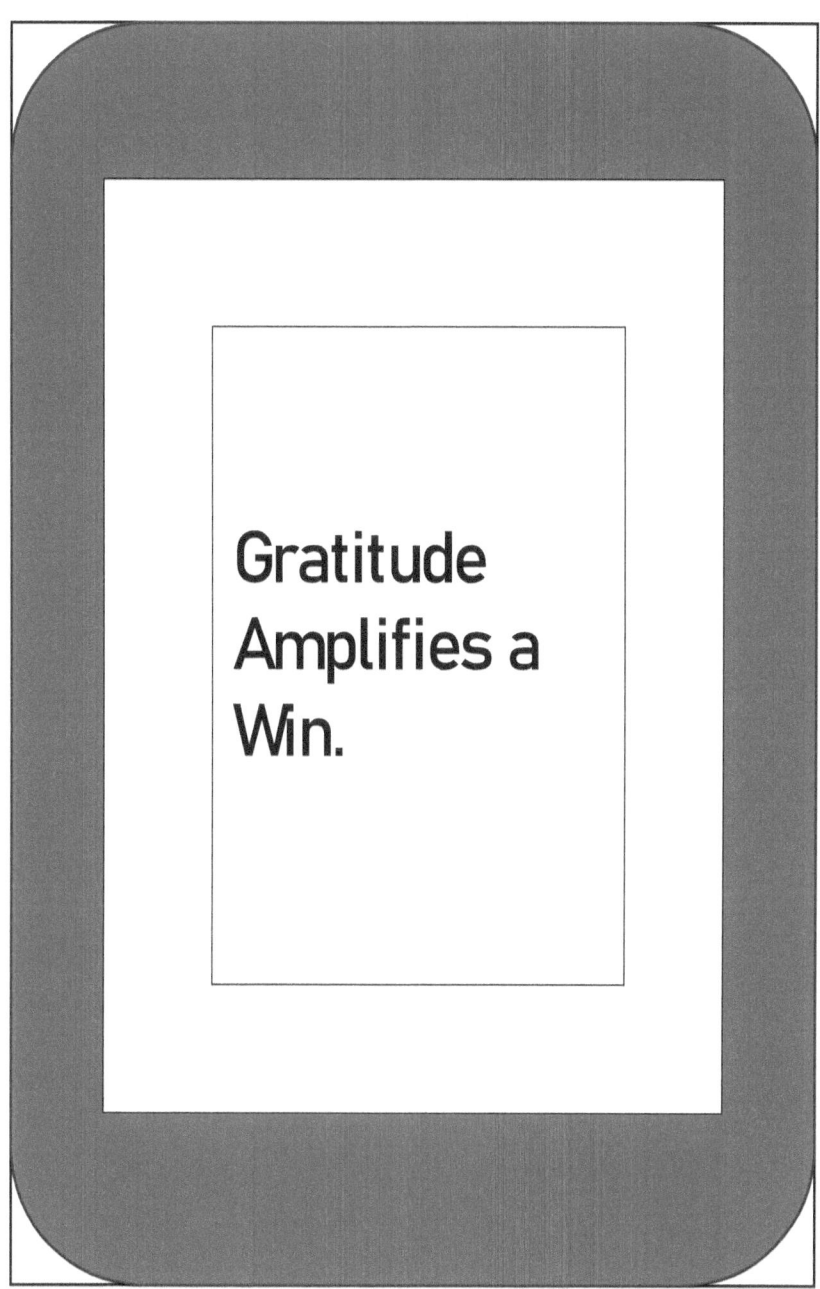

Gratitude Amplifies a Win.

EBONY D. MCPHERSON

Walk into Your Destiny with Presents.

Resources

Looking for more inspiration?
Check out this book by the same author with **Journal Included** to become inspired to dream big and think bigger.

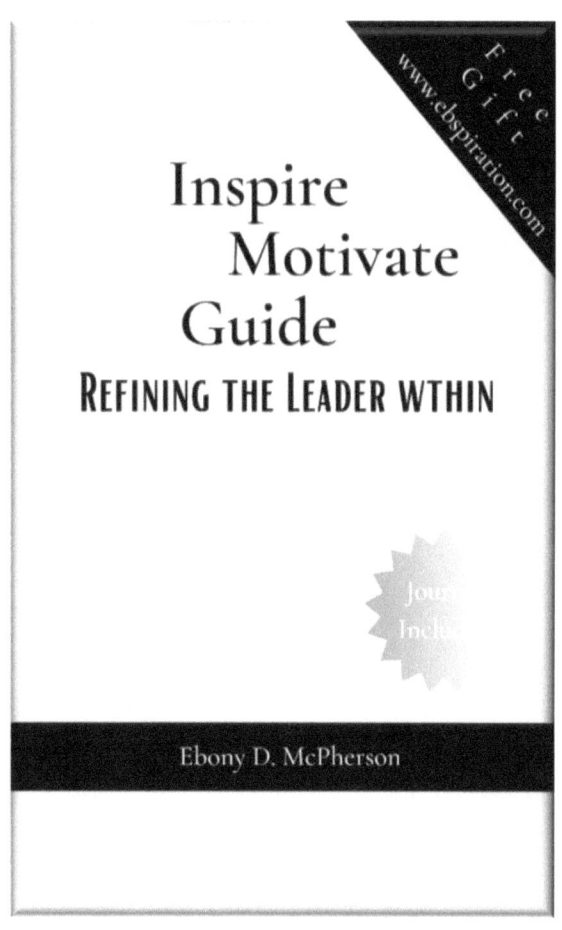

ABOUT AUTHOR

Ebony D. McPherson

Ebony is a new up and coming business lifestyle development author and transformational speaker. The inspiration for this book derived from her of the greatest influences in world culture, some of which includes Maya Angelou,  Oprah Winfrey and Michelle Obama. This book serves as an extension in her career endeavors to impact and support those aspiring to become a positive influence throughout the world. Including this one, her first book, ***Inspire Motivate Guide: Refining the Leader Within*** was the first step to many in leaving behind a trailblazing impact. Though Ebony spends her days diligently preparing for opportunities to be of greater service to her community, her pride and joy lies in maintaining a thriving private family life in preparation for the generations to come.

www.ingramcontent.com/pod-product-compliance
Lightning Source LLC
Chambersburg PA
CBHW031923240526
45464CB00022B/670